Visit the SOUTHWEST

By Kathryn Walton

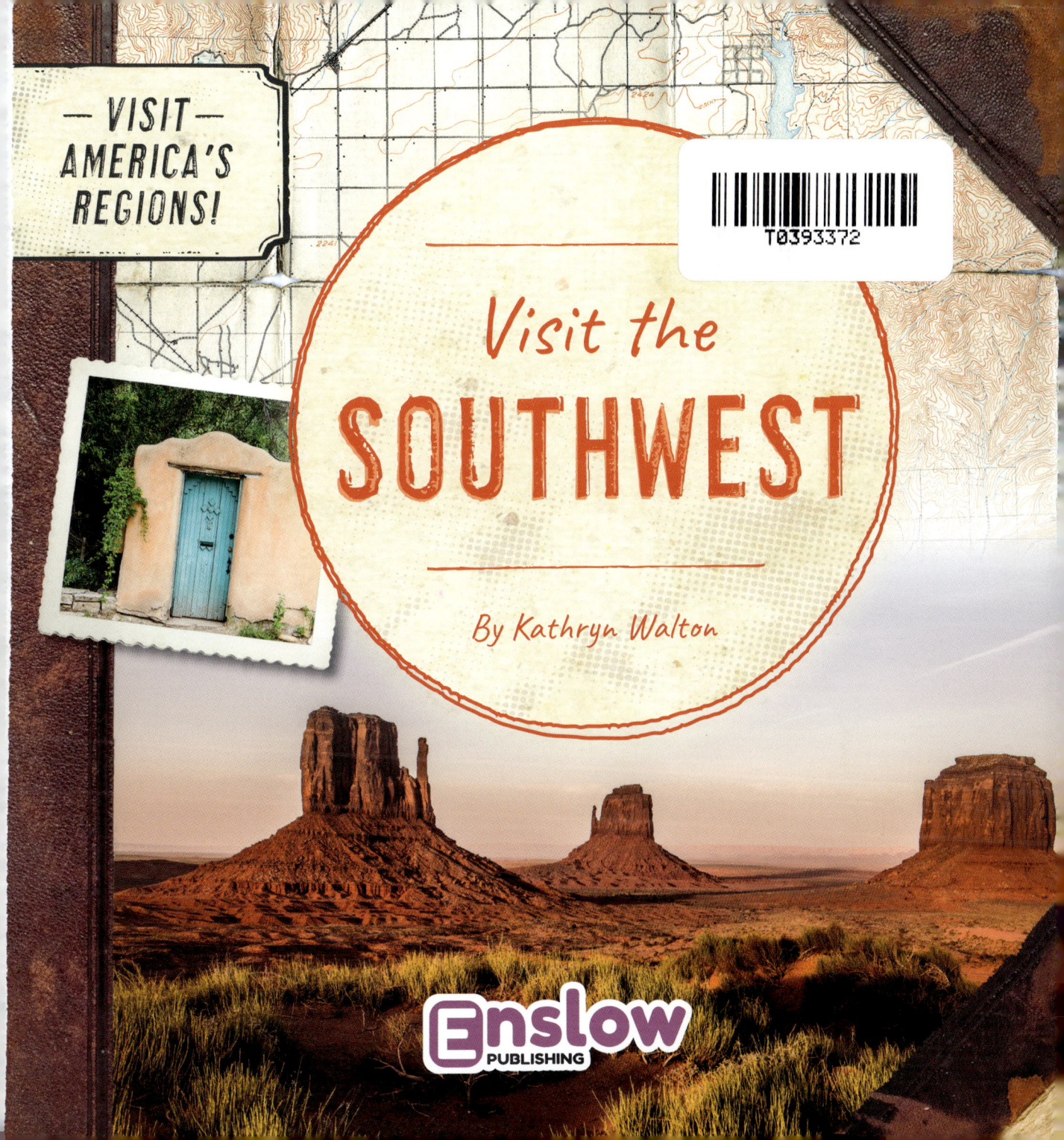

Enslow PUBLISHING

Please visit our website, www.enslow.com. For a free color catalog of all our high-quality books, call toll free 1-800-398-2504 or fax 1-877-980-4454.

Library of Congress Cataloging-in-Publication Data
Names: Walton, Kathryn.
Title: Visit the southwest / Kathryn Walton.
Description: New York : Enslow Publishing, 2024. | Series: Visit America's regions! | Includes glossary and index.
Identifiers: ISBN 9781978537620 (pbk.) | ISBN 9781978537637 (library bound) | ISBN 9781978537644 (ebook)
Subjects: LCSH: Southwestern States–Description and travel–Juvenile literature. | Southwestern States–History–Juvenile literature. | Southwestern States–Juvenile literature.
Classification: LCC F785.7 W35 2024 | DDC 976–dc23

Published in 2024 by
Enslow Publishing
2544 Clinton Street
Buffalo, NY 14224

Portions of this work were originally authored by Kathleen Connors and published as *Let's Explore The Southwest*. All new material in this edition is authored by Kathryn Walton.

Designer: Claire Wrazin
Editor: Natalie Humphrey

Photo credits: Series art (leather spine and corners) nevodka/Shutterstock.com, (map) Karin Hildebrand Lau/Shutterstock.com, (stamped boxes) lynea/Shutterstock.com, (old paper) Siam SK/Shutterstock.com, (vintage photo frame) shyshak roman/Shutterstock.com, (visitor's guide paper background) Andrey_Kuzmin/Shutterstock.com; cover, p. 1 (main) Steve Rosset/Shutterstock.com; cover, p. 1 (inset) Jim Ekstrand/Shutterstock.com; pp. 5, 21 (map) pingebat/Shutterstock.com; pp. 6, 16 (arrows) Elina Li/Shutterstock.com; p. 7 (main) Images by Dr. Alan Lipkin/Shutterstock.com, (inset) Nadia Yong/Shutterstock.com; p. 9 Beth Ruggiero-York/Shutterstock.com; p. 11 Jeffrey M. Frank/Shutterstock.com; p. 13 Manuela Durson/Shutterstock.com; p. 14 etorres/Shutterstock.com; p. 15 Paul Brady Photography/Shutterstock.com; p. 16 f11photo/Shutterstock.com; p. 17 Barackandur/Shutterstock.com; p. 18 Helena GARCIA HUERTAS/Shutterstock.com; p. 19 Marek Masik/Shutterstock.com.

Printed in the United States of America

CPSIA compliance information: Batch #CWENS24: For further information contact Enslow Publishing at 1-800-398-2504.

Find us on

CONTENTS

Words in the glossary appear in **bold** type the first time they are used in the text.

WELCOME TO THE SOUTHWEST

The Southwest **region** is known for its hot and dry weather, but there's more to this region than just that! Native American people still living in the Southwest have had a strong **influence** on southwestern **culture**. These cultures, combined with the influence of the Spanish settlers, made the Southwest what it is today.

From the bright lights of movie studios in Los Angeles, California, to hikes through the Rocky Mountains and everything in between, there's something for everyone in the Southwest.

Arizona, Southern California, Colorado, Nevada, New Mexico, Oklahoma, Texas, and Utah are all part of the Southwest.

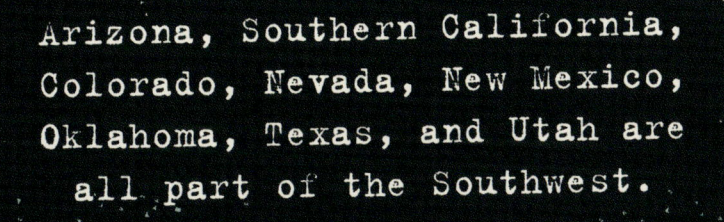

NEVADA

UTAH

COLORADO

CALIFORNIA

ARIZONA

NEW MEXICO

OKLAHOMA

PACIFIC OCEAN

TEXAS

• VISITOR'S GUIDE •

VISITORS TO THE SOUTHWEST CAN GET A TASTE OF THE WILD WEST! THROUGHOUT THE REGION, VISITORS CAN RIDE HORSES, CAMP IN THE DESERT, AND LEARN HOW COWBOYS USED TO LIVE.

THE ROCKY MOUNTAINS

Parks and trails in the Rocky Mountains are popular stops on any southwestern road trip! They're some of the main features of the region. The Colorado **Plateau** offers amazing scenery too. The red-colored rocks of its cliffs are popular with hikers and climbers.

Petrified Forest National Park in northeast Arizona has many trees that have been petrified. Visitors can also see Native American art carved, or cut into, the rocks there.

> Though dry, the Southwest has several national forests and national grasslands within its states.

• VISITOR'S GUIDE •

PETRIFICATION IS THE ACT OF WOOD TURNING INTO STONE. AFTER WOOD HAS BEEN BURIED FOR A LONG TIME, **MINERALS** SLOWLY HARDEN INSIDE OF THE PLANT'S CELLS. THE WOOD DIES AWAY, AND THE MINERALS ARE LEFT BEHIND.

RIVERS IN THE SOUTHWEST

There are two major rivers in the Southwest. The Colorado River flows through Colorado, Utah, New Mexico, Nevada, Arizona, and California in the Southwest. It starts in Rocky Mountain National Park and runs 1,450 miles (2,333 km).

The Rio Grande divides Texas and Mexico and flows into the Gulf of Mexico. In southwest Texas, you can visit Big Bend National Park, named after a bend in the Rio Grande. There are 150 miles (241 km) of hiking trails in this park.

COLORADO RIVER

The Colorado River flows through the Grand Canyon. Many people go **rafting** on this part of the Colorado River.

• VISITOR'S GUIDE •

AT THE FOUR CORNERS MONUMENT, YOU CAN STAND IN NEW MEXICO, ARIZONA, COLORADO, AND UTAH AT THE SAME TIME!

NATIVE AMERICAN PEOPLES OF THE SOUTHWEST

The Southwest wouldn't be what it is today without the Native American people who lived there for thousands of years. Some of the largest groups of Native people include the Pueblo, Navajo, and Apache. Today, more than 20 percent of Native Americans in the United States live in this region.

The Navajo have lived in the Southwest for between 800 and 1,000 years. The Navajo Nation **Reservation** found near the Four Corners is the largest reservation in the country!

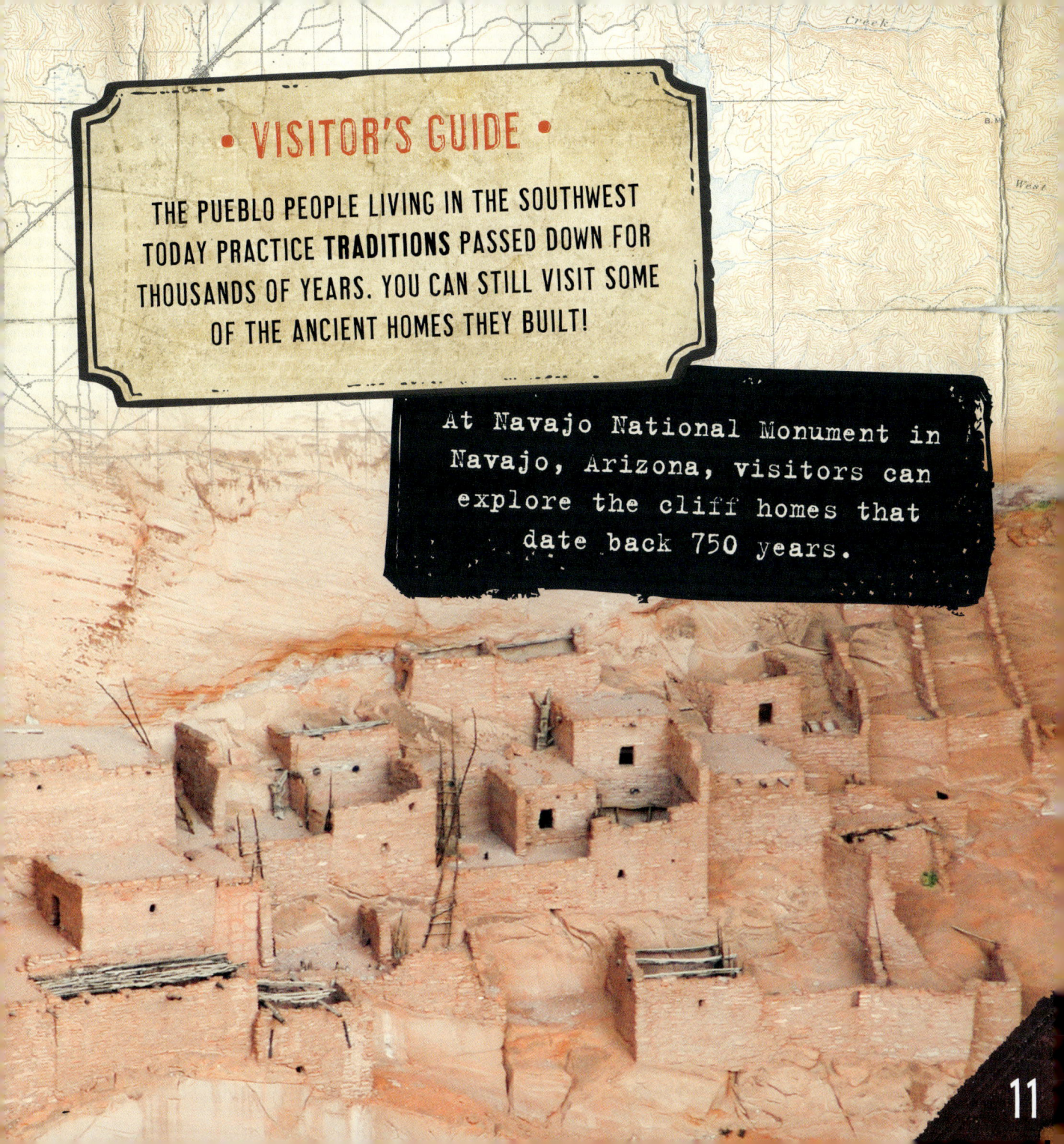

THE PUEBLO PEOPLE LIVING IN THE SOUTHWEST TODAY PRACTICE **TRADITIONS** PASSED DOWN FOR THOUSANDS OF YEARS. YOU CAN STILL VISIT SOME OF THE ANCIENT HOMES THEY BUILT!

At Navajo National Monument in Navajo, Arizona, visitors can explore the cliff homes that date back 750 years.

SPANISH SETTLERS

In the mid-1500s, Spanish settlers began moving into the Southwest. They set up **missions** in California, Arizona, and New Mexico. Later, current-day California, Nevada, Utah, Arizona, and parts of Colorado and New Mexico were all ruled by Mexico. Mexico won its independence, or freedom, from Spain in 1820 and ruled the area until 1848.

It's common to hear Spanish spoken in the Southwest region today. Knowing a few words and phrases in Spanish can help you out on your trip!

• VISITOR'S GUIDE •

VISITORS CAN STOP BY SAN XAVIER DEL BAC MISSION IN TUCSON, ARIZONA, TODAY! IT IS THE OLDEST EUROPEAN BUILDING STILL STANDING IN ARIZONA.

Visitors to the Southwest can see the ruins of many other Spanish missions.

RUINS AT TUMACACORI MISSION IN ARIZONA

CULTURAL INFLUENCES

The Spanish and Native American influence in the Southwest can be seen in much of its culture. Buildings and homes in Southwestern cities are often modeled after the Pueblo people's adobe style. Art from this region commonly features Native American stories and ideas.

Southwestern food combines the cultures of its past. One of the most popular food styles is Tex-Mex. This food, like tacos, burritos, beans, and fresh salsa, combines Mexican cuisine with the more American tastes of the Southwest.

THE PALACE OF THE GOVERNORS

PALACE OF THE GOVERNORS

• VISITOR'S GUIDE •

ADOBE STYLE HOUSES HAVE THICK WALLS THAT HELP TO KEEP HOT AIR OUT AND COOL AIR IN. THEY ARE OFTEN MADE OF MUD, CLAY, OR STRAW BRICKS.

The Palace of the Governors in Santa Fe, New Mexico, is an adobe-style house built in the early 17th century. It's used as a historical museum today!

TEXAS

Even Texas's name has roots in Spanish and Native American culture! Texas comes from the Native American word for "friends" or "allies." This word became tejas when spelled by the Spanish and later became Texas!

Texas is full of fun places to visit. San Antonio is one of the most visited places in Texas as the location of the Alamo. From 1835 to 1836, Texas fought for independence from Mexico. The Alamo was an old Spanish mission that became an important battle site.

THE ALAMO >

With a population of over 2.2 million people, Houston, Texas, is the fourth-largest city in the United States.

• VISITOR'S GUIDE •

AUSTIN, TEXAS, CALLS ITSELF THE LIVE MUSIC CAPITAL OF THE WORLD. THERE ARE OVER 200 PLACES IN THE CITY WHERE VISITORS CAN SEE LIVE MUSIC!

LOS ANGELES, CALIFORNIA

Los Angeles, California, has many things for visitors to do and see. One popular spot for visitors is the La Brea Tar Pits and Museum. This museum features open tar pits still bubbling outside. Many fossils are still being found in the La Brea Tar Pits today!

Movie lovers won't want to miss one of the many movie studio tours in Los Angeles. Visitors can take a tour through Universal Studios, Warner Bros., Paramount Pictures, and more!

Los Angeles is one of the biggest cities in the United States—and North America—with a population of 3.8 million people.

FAMOUS SOUTHWESTERN FACES

There are many famous people from the Southwest! Presidents Lyndon B. Johnson and Dwight D. Eisenhower were both born in Texas. The singer Beyoncé was also born in Texas. Billie Eilish, among many other singers and actors, is from Los Angeles!

From cultural spots to amazing nature, there's no end to the fun you can have in the Southwest! You won't want to miss a moment of a trip through this region.

• VISITOR'S GUIDE •

TO SEE MORE OF THE SOUTHWEST, WHY NOT TAKE A RIDE IN A HOT AIR BALLOON? THE LARGEST HOT AIR BALLOON **FESTIVAL** IN THE WORLD IS HELD IN ALBUQUERQUE, NEW MEXICO.

MORE THINGS TO SEE IN THE SOUTHWEST

Check out more places to stop on your trip through the Southwest!

GRIFFITH OBSERVATORY

Found near Los Angeles, California, the Griffith Observatory is free to explore! Visitors can tour the many displays about space inside.

BUC-EE'S

This store and gas station has many locations around the South and Southwest. But the Buc-ee's in Katy, Texas, has a 255-foot (78 m) long car wash. It's the longest in the world!

NEVADA

UTAH

COLORADO

CALIFORNIA

ARIZONA

NEW MEXICO

TEXAS

PACIFIC OCEAN

TAOS PUEBLO

The Native American community found in this part of New Mexico has been living there for the past 1,000 years.

SAN ANTONIO'S RIVER WALK

This walk along the San Antonio River in San Antonio, Texas, is one of the most popular stops in the state!

GLOSSARY

culture: The beliefs and ways of life of a group of people.

festival: A public event usually hosted every year to celebrate something.

influence: To have an effect on.

mineral: Matter in the ground that forms rocks.

mission: A building used by Christian missionaries to try and teach people about the Christian faith.

plateau: A large area of land with raised sides and a level top.

reservation: Land set aside by the U.S. government for Native Americans.

rafting: Traveling in a flat boat with low sides.

region: A large area of land that has features that make it different from nearby areas of land.

tradition: Having to do with long-practiced customs.

FOR MORE INFORMATION

Books

Harrison, Audrey. *Arizona*. Minneapolis, MN: Core Library, 2023.

Jacobson, Bray. *The Grand Canyon*. Buffalo, NY: Gareth Stevens Publishing, 2023.

Websites

Britannica Kids: The Southwest
kids.britannica.com/kids/article/The-Southwest/489352
Learn more facts about the climate, geography, and settlement of the Southwest.

National Geographic Kids: Native People of the American Southwest
www.kids.nationalgeographic.com/history/article/native-people-of-the-american-southwest
Find out more about the people who lived in the American Southwest before European settlers.

INDEX